AF413399

HIP HOP A2Z 50 YEARS AND COUNTING 1973-∞

Illustrated by
Robb Frostbyte King
M Paul Perry
Troop Thomas
Robert "Suave" Waugh II

CONTENTS

FOREWORD

This publication is intended to persuade the reader to believe that the development and advancement of Hip-Hop culture is a phenomenal cultural revolution. Hip-Hop is more than rap music. It is intended to present facts to support Hip-Hop as a movement of peace and unity through creative expression. This publication is intended to document Hip-Hop's rise from a local, condemned fad to arguably the most influential culture in the United States and throughout the entire world. This publication is intended to present important facts that contributed to the development and spread of Hip-Hop culture. This publication is intended to tell a story of triumph. This publication tells a story of how marginalized and diverse inner-city youth established a culture that is non-discriminating racially, socially, economically, or through self-identity. Hip-Hop practitioners around the globe make it the most diverse culture around.

The content of this publication is suitable for everyone, however beginning or struggling readers may need a read-aloud.

"Hip-Hop didn't invent anything. Hip-Hop reinvented everything." **Grand Master Caz.**

PAN-
AFRICAN
CULTURE

A1
IS FOR AFRICAN AND PAN-AFRICAN

African culture is heavily embedded in Hip-Hop culture. African and Pan-African culture is characterized by expressive spoken words, language, and songs. African and Pan-African culture is distinguished by energetic and synchronized dance. African art is known to be very colorful. African and Pan-African art embodies a wide variety of content. Also, this art often contains the manipulation of geometric shapes to create the illusion of three dimensions.

The drum is sacred to African and Pan-African culture. The drum beat is also the cornerstone of Hip-Hop music. Hip-Hop music is riddled with poetic storytelling. The call and response is a signature practice during live performances. Hip-Hop music contains rhythmic cadences and chants similar to that of African tribal rituals. Break dancing and choreographed Hip-Hop dance teams embody the energy and expressiveness seen in African dance. Graffiti art is very bold and colorful. It is often used to pay homage and bring consciousness, or awareness to a particular issue in society. African and Pan-African culture has the strongest influence on Hip-Hop culture. Hip-Hop culture is one of the most influential cultures in America and across the globe.

Aa2
IS FOR AFRIKA BAMBAATAA

Afrika Bambaataa has played a major role in Hip-Hop culture becoming an American and international phenomenon. He is known as the Godfather of Hip-Hop culture. He is one-third of the Hip Hop Holy Trinity. Bambaataa is a Hip Hop DJ from the South Bronx who gained notoriety for throwing block parties. Afrika Bambaataa was known as a high-ranking gang member. He decided to use Hip-Hop as a platform for social uplift and a cultural movement. He repurposed his street gang into the Universal Zulu Nation. Bambaataa established a motto of "Peace, Love, Unity, and Having Fun". Bambaataa is credited for spreading the gospel of the four elements of Hip-Hop, which are deejaying, break dancing, emceeing, and graffiti art. Afrika Bambaataa is credited for spreading Hip-Hop culture from the projects and parks of the South Bronx to the clubs of Manhattan and Europe.

AFRIKA
BAMBAATAA

B-BOY
B-GIRL

B1
IS FOR BREAK DANCING
(B-BOYING & B-GIRLING)

Break dancing is a very popular style of dance in the United States and throughout the entire world. Break dancing began in New York. It may be considered the spirit of Hip-Hop culture. Break dancing is one of the four primary elements that provide the foundation of Hip-Hop culture. In the early 1970s break dancing came into existence as a new style of street deejaying provided the platform for a more energetic and acrobatic style of dance. DJ Kool Herc pioneered a style of deejaying in which the breakbeats of the most popular songs were emphasized. The breakbeat is packed with drum patterns and heavy bass, this new style of street dance was named break dancing. Many gangs in New York City had dance crews. As Afrika Bambaataa pushed for Hip Hop to be a social movement, these dance crews began competitive dance battles instead of violent confrontations. The Rock Steady Crew formed by Joe Torres and Jimmy D. became very popular B-boy practitioners. Today break dancing is a part of many live concerts and music videos. Many sports franchises have dance teams that feature the finest break dancers in the area. There are several world tournaments to crown the best B-boys and B-girls across the globe. Korea, Japan, Canada, and Russia have very strong break-dancing communities.

BEATBOXING

Bb2
IS FOR BEAT BOXING

Beatboxing played a significant role in the spread of Hip-Hop music to the American mainstream and beyond. The pioneers of Hip-Hop culture came from poverty-stricken urban areas in New York City. Beatboxing is a prime example of the ingenuity of early Hip Hoppers. Aspiring DJs and MCs lacked the resources to obtain turntables, beat machines, and other musical instruments. Die-hard enthusiasts began using their lips, tongue, nose, and throat to create rhythmic beats and sound effects. A manipulation of the larynx and hand claps along with a controlled diaphragm was a suitable substitute for instruments and technology. Buff "the Human Beatbox" of the Fat Boys is a beatbox pioneer. Two of the most popular beatboxers who contributed to the advancement of Hip-Hop from the street corners into mainstream America are Doug E. Fresh and Biz Markie. Fresh is known for his beatbox on the track "La Di Da Di", which made him an international star along with Slick Rick. He would also gain mainstream notoriety from Cali Swag District's "Teach Me How to Dougie", which incorporated some of Fresh's dance moves in the performance. The late Biz Markie is probably most known for his "Just a Friend" smash hit. He pushed Hip Hop culture as a recording artist and actor.

DOUG E. FRESH

BIZ MARKIE

COKE
LA
ROCK

C1
IS FOR COKE LA ROCK

Coke La Rock can be traced to the root of Hip Hop's most popular element across the entire world, emceeing. Coke La Rock is credited by most Hip-Hop scholars as the first MC. The MC is the predecessor to the rapper. Coke La Rock was a part of DJ Kool Herc's crew. Coke La Rock began emceeing for Herc. His primary function was to use the microphone to engage the crowd in an effort to keep the party energized. He gave shoutouts and developed short clever rhymes. Coke La Rock engaged the party crowds with call and response. His style of emceeing was heavily influenced by the Jamaican tradition of toasting. Coke La Rock undeniably helped plant the seeds of the global multi-billion-dollar rap industry.

Cc2
IS FOR COMMON

Common is a Hip-Hop artist who has grabbed the attention of the American Performing Art Awards. Eminem has made some noteworthy accomplishments as well. Both of these artists are one Tony award away from the coveted EGOT. The EGOT is an acronym for Emmy, Grammy, Oscar, and Tony awards. This grand slam of awards has only been accomplished by 18 people. Common and Eminem are on the cusp of being the first Hip Hop artist to complete the EGOT. Common has three Grammy awards. He won a Grammy and an Oscar for his collaboration with John Legend titled "Glory". Common went on to collect an Emmy for the socially conscious song "Letter to the Free", making him the first Hip-Hop artist to win an Emmy, Grammy, and Oscar. Eminem would follow suit when his performance at the halftime show of Super Bowl LVI earned him an Emmy. Eminem has 15 Grammy awards and one Oscar for "Lose Yourself".

COMMON

Eminem

DJ

D1
IS FOR DJ (DEEJAYING)

The DJ has been around since well before the emergence of Hip-Hop. However, the emergence of Hip-Hop deejaying is the genesis of a cultural explosion that has impacted the entire world. Deejaying is one of the four primary elements of Hip- Hop culture. It may be considered the pulse of Hip-Hop culture. DJ stands for disc Jockey. It is the primary function of the DJ to play the music selections to motivate the crowd of party participants to dance and sing enthusiastically. As DJ Kool Herc developed a new technique of deejaying, it was the catalyst for other aspiring DJs to further develop techniques. Grand Master Flash developed quick mixes and concentrated on smooth transitions. Grand Wizard Theodore is credited with introducing scratching and backspinning. The DJ was the most popular person in the early stages of Hip-Hop. The DJ provided the platform for B-boying, b-girling, and emceeing. Hip Hop began in house parties, but it spilt into the parks and clubs throughout New York. Hip-Hop started out as a condemned urban subculture. However, the DJs would push forward as the soundtrack of one of the most influential cultures in America and throughout the world.

THE HIP HOP DECLARATION OF PEACE

Dd2
IS FOR DECLARATION OF PEACE

The Hip-Hop Declaration of Peace was presented to the United Nations Organization in New York on May 16th 2001. This declaration recognizes Hip-Hop as an international culture of peace and prosperity. The document is composed of 18 principles. The intended purpose of the document is to highlight the Hip-Hop movement as a positive movement and cultural, global phenomenon. Some major contributors to the declaration are KRS-One, Ralph Mc Daniels, Pop Master Fabel, and Harry Allen. The document was signed by over 300 advocates, which includes agencies and U.N. delegates.

ELEMENTS
OF HIP·HOP CULTURE
SPRAY
CAN

E1

IS FOR ELEMENTS OF HIP-HOP CULTURE

The elements of Hip-Hop serve as the core of the culture's ascension into arguably the most influential culture in America and beyond. In the early stages of Hip-Hop, it seems as though its foundational elements began to simultaneously align. In urban areas throughout the United States, minorities have been neglected and deprived by mainstream America and popular culture. These elements would prove to be a platform for the economically grim. This emerging new culture embraced audacious, individual expression. Hip-Hop culture gave the impoverished a creative and artistic voice on social and political issues. Deejaying, break dancing, emceeing, and graffiti art were established as four primary elements that function as the pillars of Hip-Hop culture. Afrika Bambaataa pushed the elements and advocated for knowledge as the 5th element. Hip-Hop scholars offer varying lists of elements of Hip-Hop. Currently, the Temple of Hip-Hop identifies 9 elements of Hip-Hop.

ELEMENTS OF HIP-HOP

1.   Breaking

2.   Emceeing

3.   Graffiti Art

4.   Deejaying

5.   Beat Boxing

6.   Street Fashion

7.   Street Language

8.   Street Knowledge

9.   Street Entrepreneurialism

$
STREET
ENTREPRENEURIALISM
SEDGWICK AVE.
CEDAR PARK
UNITED STATES OF AMERICA
100

Ee2
IS FOR ENTREPRENEURIALISM

Entrepreneurialism is an element of Hip-Hop culture that has established it as a multi-billion dollar industry internationally. As the popularity of Hip-Hop expanded, many of its elements created business opportunities. Advertisement, promotions, management, video, and music production opportunities began to spring up. Hip-Hop entrepreneurs would advance to clothing lines, movie production, record labels, and sports franchises. These have become common endeavors for Hip-Hop entrepreneurs. Some of the most successful Hip Hop entrepreneurs include Russell Simmons, Luke, P. Diddy, Master P, Snoop Dogg, Dr. Dre, Ice Cube, and 50 Cent.

STARTER
71
FRESH
STREET
FASHION
FB

F1
IS FOR FASHION

Hip-Hop fashion is sought after throughout the entire world. Street fashion is an element of Hip Hop culture. In the 1980s Hip-Hop gained steam in popularity. The expanding population in this blossoming new phenomenon became very influential to a particular footwear, clothing apparel, name brands, jewellery, and hairstyles. Run DMC signed a million-dollar endorsement deal with Adidas in the mid-1980s. Dapper Dan became notorious for his customized, designer apparel. Clothing lines such as Fubu, Karl Kani, Walker Wear, and Baby Phat were established to outfit the expanding Hip-Hop market. Today's Hip-Hop entrepreneurs and moguls push Hip- Hop fashion through multimillion-dollar endorsement deals, partnerships, and clothing lines. Entrepreneurs like P. Diddy and Ye have become billionaires with the help of fashion. Ye once had several fashion partnerships, and he collaborated with the late Virgil Abloh to spread street fashion abroad. P. Diddy made his imprint on Hip-Hop fashion with the establishment of Sean Jean. Diddy is a recipient of the Council of Fashion Designers of America award. Pharrell Williams landed the role as Men's Creative Director for Louis Vuitton. Former international model Kimora Lee Simmons helped to launch Baby Phat to target female urban fashion.

THE SWATCH WATCH NEW YORK CITY
FRESH FESTIVAL '84
TONIGHT'S PERFORMING ACTS
THE FAT BOYS
WHODINI
NEWCLEUS
UPTOWN EXPRESS
MAG FORCE/SWATCH BREAKERS
THE DYNAMIC BREAKERS
RUN D.M.C.
OAKLAND COLISEUM
SUNDAY DEC 2, 1984

Ff2
IS FOR FRESH FEST TOUR

Hip-Hop tours would become another vehicle to spread Hip Hop culture beyond the house parties, street parks, and clubs. The Fresh Fest Tour was the first large-scale Hip-Hop tour. It was preceded by the Kitchen Tour in 1982. The Fresh Festival was headlined by Run-D.M.C. The tour was a major success, grossing over $3 million. A percentage of the proceeds went to benefit the United Negro College Fund. The Fresh Festival would go on to be an annual event touring through arenas in most of the major cities throughout the nation.

ART
GRAFFITI
Hip Hop

G1
IS FOR GRAFFITI ART

Graffiti art is popular throughout major cities across the world. Graffiti, or street art, is one of the primary elements that serve as the pillars of Hip-Hop culture. In the early stages of Hip-Hop culture, graffiti may have been deemed the most rebellious aspect of Hip-Hop culture. Primarily, graffiti art was tagged on trains and large buildings. Therefore, the art form was illegal and considered vandalism. Graffiti was notable throughout large cities on the East and West Coast. Early use of graffiti marked territory for gang activity. In the late 60's and early 70's impoverished artists began to create graffiti pieces that were an opportunity for individual expressions. This art form was very prominent in Philadelphia and New York. In New York, many styles of graffiti art began to materialize. Fab 5 Freddy and organizations such as United Graffiti Artists advocated to give substance to graffiti as an art form. TAKI 183, PHASE, SAMO, and Fab 5 Freddy are a few graffiti pioneers. Today, graffiti is used on murals to honor the dead, political satire, social awareness, self-promotion, and advertisements on buildings, billboards, apparel, and canvases throughout the entire world.

FAB 5 FREDDY

Gg2
IS FOR GRANDMASTER FLASH

Grand Master Flash is a DJ from the South Bronx New York City that helped transcend Hip Hop culture beyond an urban, street culture. He is one-third of the Hip Hop Holy Trinity. Grandmaster Flash is a native of Barbados who was raised in the South Bronx. Flash was known for his expertise in electronics. He put his skills to use by perfecting techniques such as backspinning, cutting, and scratching. This contributed to the distinctive sounds of Hip Hop music. He would go on to organize the group Grand Master Flash and the Furious Five. Flash and the Furious Five ushered in a distinct style of rap, with lyrics that described the harsh realities of urban lifestyles in New York and beyond. The work of Grandmaster Flash and the Furious Five's musical contributions have definitely contributed to the genre's influence on mainstream America, further solidifying Hip-Hop as a cultural movement. Grandmaster Flash and the Furious Five were the first Hip-Hop artists inducted into the Rock & Roll Hall of Fame in 2007 punctuating their impact on popular culture.

GRAND MASTER
FLASH

H1
IS FOR HIP-HOP CULTURE

Hip-Hop culture is a way of life that is arguably the most influential culture around the world. Remnants of Hip Hop culture can be traced back to some large urban areas of the 1940s, 50s, & 60s. The elements of Hip-Hop began to align in a more evident and pervasive way in the early 1970s. Hip-Hop scholars and historians acknowledge August 11, 1973, as the birthday of Hip Hop culture. At 1520 Sedgwick Avenue, the Bronx, New York a young DJ by the name of Kool Herc had a party. It was at this party that this young intuitive D.J. unveiled the deejaying technique of extending the break beats using two turntables. This new style proved to be a catalyst to ignite an urban cultural phenomenon that attracted Blacks and Latinos. Many of the early participants and pioneers of the Hip-Hop culture had Jamaican, Puerto Rican, Bahamian, and Barbadian roots. This merge of urban ethnicity along with burgeoning new ways of individual expression culminated in the development of Hip-Hop culture. This movement of expression which materialized in the form of music, dance, and art was intended to be a movement of unity. The term Hip-Hop originated around 1978 by Keith "Cowboy" Wiggins (a member of Grandmaster Flash and the Furious Five). It was made popular and spread by Lovebug Starski and DJ Hollywood. Today, the Hip-Hop culture has penetrated every race, ethnicity, and creed throughout the globe.

A DJ KOOL HERC PARTY

★ ⁙ BACK TO SCHOOL JAM ★ ★

PLACE: 1520 SEDGWICK AVE. "REC ROOM"

DATE: AUGUST 11, 1973

TIME: 9:00 PM TO 4:00 AM.

ADMISSION: $.25 LADIES ♡
$.50 FELLAS

GIVEN BY: KOOL HERC

SCHOOL'S STILL OUT

SPECIAL GUEST: COCO, CINDY C., KLARK K., TIMMY T

HiP-HOP
HOLLYWOOD
WALK OF FAME

Hh2
IS FOR THE HOLLYWOOD WALK OF FAME

The Hollywood Walk of Fame is a significant honor, because Hollywood is considered to be the show-business capital of the world. Hollywood attracts aspiring entertainers from every corner of the globe. Therefore, to be honored with a star on the Hollywood Walk of Fame is a distinguished tribute. The Walk of Fame has six categories: motion pictures, television, radio, recording, live theatre/performance, and sports entertainment. All nominee's contributions to the community and civic-oriented participation are taken into consideration. There are 13 Hip Hop artists that have stars on the Hollywood Walk of Fame.

Queen Latifah	2006
Sean "Diddy" Combs	2008
Pharrell Williams	2014
LL Cool J	2016
Pitbull	2016
Ice Cube	2017
Snoop Dogg	2018
Cypress Hill	2019
50 Cent	2020
Missy Elliot	2021
Ice-T	2023
Ludacris	2023
Tupac Shakur	2023

I1
IS FOR ICE CUBE

Ice Cube is a Hip-Hop artist who uses his platform to impact the American pop culture as well as the global Hip-Hop scene. Ice Cube gained notoriety as a member of the controversial rap group NWA, where he served as a rapper and a writer for the group. Ice Cube is known for speaking out on social injustice and police brutality. Ice Cube would sever ties with NWA and make his way to the Hollywood big screen as an actor, writer, director, and producer. He launched Cube Vision which is responsible for *Friday* and *Barbershop* series of projects. He has been involved with hundreds of movies and recordings in some capacity or another. Ice Cube earned an Image Award in 2011 for his role in *Are We There Yet?* In June of 2017, Ice Cube received a star on the Hollywood Walk of Fame. Ice Cube recently made history as the first black owner of a sports league with the BIG3 basketball league. Ice Cube is a dedicated philanthropist. Cube supports funding for Autism Speaks, and he supported hospitals in the fight against Coronavirus during the pandemic.

ICE CUBE

Ii2
IS FOR ICE T

Ice T is a Hip-Hop artist who uses his platform to impact the American pop culture as well as the international Hip-Hop scene. Ice T began his career as a DJ and rapper. He would go on to portray a B-boy in the movie *Breakin* in 1984, a movie which depicts Los Angeles' early impact on the Hip-Hop scene. Ice-T's career continues to flourish as a recording artist and an actor. Ice T has over a dozen albums and compilations. He earned a Grammy award for his contributions to a collaboration with Quincy Jones. He has hundreds of projects as an actor on the big screen and television. Ice T earned an Image Award twice. He earned the award in 2002 and 1996 for his roles in *Law & Order* and *New York Undercover* respectively. Ice T was honored with a star on the Hollywood Walk of Fame in 2023. Ice T is a known supporter of the American Heart Association and the American Humane Association. He has also supported causes for U.S. veterans.

J1
IS FOR JACK THE RAPPER

The Jack the Rapper was a black music convention that helped popularize Hip-Hop music in the American mainstream. Jack "the Rapper" Gibson was a radio DJ at the first black-owned radio station. In 1949 WERD radio station was established in Atlanta, Georgia. The late Joseph Deighton Gibson Jr. was hired as a DJ. He would go on to be known as Jockey Jack, and eventually, Jack the Rapper would be his most popular alias. Jack became popular for his broadcast delivery. His jive, or street language, made him popular among "black appeal" radio stations. He was known for talking jive and saying hip rhymes between records. By 1977, Jack decided to initiate a black music convention called the Jack the Rapper. This convention was a great platform for the black music industry to blossom. The convention had seminars, and performances, and even presented awards. By the 1980s, rap music had begun to gain popularity in the American mainstream. Along with R&B, Jazz, and Funk, Jack the Rapper embraced the rap community as well. The convention helped launch the careers of many rappers, producers, and record executives. The Jack the Rapper ran for 18 years.

Jj2
IS FOR JAY-Z

Jay-Z is a Hip-Hop artist who has significant influence on American pop culture as well as the international Hip-Hop culture. Jay-Z is the first Hip-Hop artist to earn Billionaire status. Jay-Z burst on the scene as an MC and entrepreneur in the late 1990s. Jay-Z has dozens of solo and collaborative Hip-Hop recordings, which have sold over 140 million units and earned him 24 Grammy awards. He is considered by many to be the greatest rapper ever. Jay-Z has proven to be equally as triumphant as an entrepreneur. Jay-Z capitalized off of the sale of the Tidal streaming company. His Marcy Venture Partners investment firm continues to make lucrative investments. His many business endeavors have his net worth at around $ 2.5 billion. Jay-Z supports a plethora of charities and foundations. Artists for Peace and Justice, Global Poverty Project, and Keep a Child Alive are a few. Jay-Z's Shawn Carter Foundation has paid millions of dollars for scholarships and counselling opportunities

NY
JAY-Z

K1
IS FOR KNOWLEDGE

Street knowledge is an element of Hip-Hop culture that continues to play a part in spreading its content into the mainstream. As Hip-Hop culture materialized in the streets of New York, the pioneers organized and advocated for it as a cultural movement. Identifying and teaching the elements of Hip-Hop shaped its expression socially, politically, and economically. Spreading the knowledge of the culture generated its expansion to cities all across the United States and across the globe. Hip-Hop pioneer Afrika Bambaataa has always advocated for consciousness and knowledge of Hip-Hop culture. KRS-One and Chuck D of Public Enemy have been proponents of political and social knowledge as it pertains to the Hip-Hop community through music and other advocacy efforts. Congress declared November, National Hip-Hop History Month in 2021. The bill was sponsored by Congresswoman Maxine Waters, Congressman Jamaal Bowman, and Sen. Chuck Schumer. The bill was established to celebrate Hip Hop's persisting influence on American culture.

Kk2
IS FOR KOOL HERC

DJ Kool Herc is a DJ from the South Bronx, New York. Herc is the father of Hip-Hop and one-third of the Holy Trinity of Hip-Hop. Herc is a Jamaican immigrant heavily influenced by the elaborate sound systems of Jamaica. He began deejaying house parties around 1971. DJ Kool Herc became so popular that he had to begin hosting his parties at recreation centers and parks. Herc developed a style of deejaying that would prompt the Hip-Hop movement when he and his sister hosted a back-to-school party in 1973. Herc used two turn tables and played the breakbeat of the same record, thus extending the most anticipated part of the song. He called this technique the merry-go-round. DJ Kool Herc is credited for the terms B-boy B-girl for the dancers to this new style of musical expression. DJ Kool Herc is an inductee to the Rock and Roll Hall of Fame as of 2023.

KOOL
HERC

LADY PINK
PINK

L1
IS FOR LADY PINK

Lady Pink is a graffiti artist who continues to legitimize the graffiti art form throughout the U.S. and the entire world. Lady Pink was born in Ecuador and grew up in New York. Lady Pink became extremely popular among the best graffiti artists in the city around the age of 15 years old. She starred in the motion picture *Wild Style*. She had her first solo art gallery show by the age of 21. Her work has been featured in the Whitney Museum of Art and the Metropolitan Museum of Art. Lady Pink has collections of work at the Groningen Museum of Holland. Lady Pink has sold her work at premiere places such as Sotheby's. Lady Pink uses her artwork for activism. Today, many of her pieces address mental health. She has been an artist for over four decades. Lady Pink continues to create paintings on canvases and murals. She does workshops and lectures for college students all over the world.

LL is for LL Cool J

IS FOR LL COOL J

LL Cool J is a Hip-Hop superstar. LL has made an everlasting impression on mainstream pop culture as well as the global Hip-Hop community. LL began his career as a 17-year-old rapper on Def Jam Records. He immediately achieved mainstream success cementing himself as one of the premiere Hip-Hop artists. LL would go on to establish a career on the Hollywood big screen and television. LL has sold over 13 million albums. He won two Grammy awards for "Momma Said Knock You Out" in 1992 and "Hey Lover" in 1997. LL Cool J was the first Hip-Hop artist to be honored by the Kennedy Center Honors in 2017. He received a star on the Hollywood Walk of Fame in 2016. LL Cool J was inducted into the Rock & Roll Hall of Fame in 2021. He currently uses his Rock the Bells Radio XM station and the Rock the Bells Festival to promote Hip-Hop culture worldwide. LL Cool J's philanthropy includes support for CORE, Diamond Empowerment Fund, and World Vision. For over 15 years LL and his Jump & Ball foundation have provided a free basketball camp for kids ages 8-17 in his hometown of Queens.

LL COOL J

Fresh

M1

IS FOR M C (EMCEEING)

The MC has been around well before the emergence of Hip-Hop. However, the emergence of Hip-Hop emceeing has propelled the culture into a global phenomenon. Emceeing is one of the four primary elements that serve as a pillar of Hip-Hop culture. It is undeniably the voice and face of Hip-Hop culture. MC stands for master of ceremony. As Hip-Hop emceeing further developed, it is known to mean microphone controller. It is the primary function of the MC to promote the DJ while engaging the party crowd. The MC is responsible for maintaining a high energy level of the party crowd. The MC is expected to entertain and elicit excitement. As DJ Kool Herc developed a new technique of deejaying, Hip-Hop DJs and MCs began to emerge throughout New York. Coke-La-Rock, DJ Hollywood, Timmy Tim and Clark Kent are some of the pioneers of emceeing. As the Hip-Hop MCs gained notoriety, many moved from rocking block parties and clubs to making recordings to feature their skills. The MC gave rise to the Hip-Hop rapper. Hip-Hop started out as a condemned urban subculture. However, the MCs would push forward as the voice and face of one of the most influential cultures in America and throughout the world. Coke La Rock is credited as the first MC. Sha Rock is credited as the first female MC.

Mm2

IS FOR MISSY ELLIOTT

Missy Elliott is a Hip-Hop artist who has impacted mainstream America and international culture as well. Missy Elliott is one of the most dynamic and versatile Hip-Hop artists. Elliott's talents include rapping, singing, writing, and producing music. She is very popular for her music videos which highlight a more playful and colorful style of B-girling and B-boying. Her talents are not limited to Hip-Hop music. Missy Elliott has collaborated with artists from just about every popular American genre of music. She has sold over 30 million records worldwide. Missy Elliott has accumulated a long list of awards and accolades. Elliott has two American Music Awards. She has one ASCAP award. She has racked up four Grammy awards, and Missy has earned eight VMA awards. Missy Elliott has been acknowledged for her work by the Song Writers Hall of Fame. Missy Elliott received her star on the Hollywood Walk of Fame in 2021. She is a 2023 inductee to the Rock & Roll Hall of Fame. Missy Elliott is an advocate against domestic violence. She supports such charities as MusiCares and PETA.

Missy

BROOKYN
NATIONAL
TV COVERAGE

N1
IS FOR NATIONAL T.V. COVERAGE

By the early 1980's Hip Hop culture had begun to spread throughout the United States. Rap music emerged as the voice of the culture. National Television coverage would step up to play its role by broadcasting the faces of Hip-Hop culture. In October of 1980, Kurtis Blow appeared on Soul Train. This made him the first rapper to perform on National Television. In February of 1981, the Funky 4 + 1 were the musical guests on Saturday Night Live. This made them the first rap group to perform on National Television. Sha Rock, the only female MC of the crew, became the first female MC to perform on National Television with this performance. In July of 1981 ABC News' 20/20 gave Hip-Hop culture its first National Television News coverage. The ten-minute segment was hosted by Steve Fox. It covered Hip Hop's strong African-American influence. The broadcast also delves into the many origins of rapping and rhyming throughout the history of the African-American community. The segment also highlighted break dancing and rap battles as peaceful competitions among rival groups and crews. The coverage predicted that Hip-Hop would be a cultural mainstay, due to its ability to give the underprivileged a platform for creative expression.

Nn2
IS FOR NEW YORK CITY
RAP TOUR

Hip-Hop tours would become another vehicle to spread Hip-Hop culture beyond the house parties, street parks, and clubs. The New York City Rap Tour was the first international Hip-Hop tour in 1982. The tour played 12 cities in Europe. The New York City Rap Tour made 10 stops in France and two shows in England. The New York City Rap Tour played its part in spreading Hip-Hop culture. The tour had a representation of the four elements of Hip-Hop. It was not merely a rap concert. Fab 5 Freddy and Kool Lady Blue played a part in the production of the New York City Rap Tour. The tour featured Afrika Bambaataa, the Infinity Rappers, and the Rock Steady Crew. Dondi, Phase Two, and Futura 2000 were some of the graffiti artists. There have been countless numbers of successful international Hip-Hop tours to date. Recently, Kendrick Lamar's Big Steppers Tour became the highest-grossing Hip-Hop tour ever. The tour grossed over $110.9 million stopping in 73 cities across the world including Canada, Europe, Australia, Japan, and South America. Kendrick also made history on April 26, 2018, when his album *Damn* won the Pulitzer Prize in the music category. This accomplishment is considered by many to be Hip-Hop's most distinguished accomplishment.

KENDRICK
LAMAR

O1
IS FOR OJ CAR SERVICE

The OJ car service played a role in spreading the buzzing underground sounds of Hip-Hop throughout the five boroughs of New York. Owners of luxury cars would allow cab companies to dispatch them to paying customers who wanted to ride in style for a particular occasion. This system was a primitive version of Uber. Many cab companies offered the service, however, OJ Cab Company became most popular around 1976. Perhaps, OJ became the powerhouse due to their reliability and variety of luxury vehicles available. The Oldsmobile 98, Lincoln Town Car, Buick Park Avenue, and the Cadillac were some of the most popular. Many of the Hip- Hop DJs began to make personal mix tapes for the OJ drivers to play in their vehicles, spreading the underground sounds of Hip-Hop. Passengers felt prestigious pulling up to an event or location in the luxury OJ vehicle with the sounds of unique artistry blasting on the car stereo. Big Bank Hank rhymes, "A skip jive what can I say? I can't fit'em all inside my OJ," on "Rapper's Delight." Slick Rick rapped, "Why don't you give me some play? And we can go cruising in my OJ," on the Hip-Hop classic "La Di Da Di."

OLYMPUS

Oo2
IS FOR OLYMPIC GAMES

The Olympic Games are a global athletic competition. It is by far the most prestigious and distinguished global athletic competition. The Olympic Games can be categorized as a celebratory competition with over 400 events and more than 200 participating nations. Hip-Hop has penetrated the world's most popular and prestigious competition. The Paris 2024 Olympics will host the first break dancing competitions. The break dancing competition will comprise two events. There will be a competition for b-boys and b-girls. The b-boys and b-girls will participate in solo battles in a field of 16 competitors. Break dancing began as a local street competition, and in the span of 50 years, it has made its way into the most popular international competition in the world.

P1

"PARENTS JUST DON'T UNDERSTAND."

The Grammy Awards are the most prestigious awards in the music industry. Ten years after Hip-Hop music burst into the American music industry, Hip-Hop has increased its influence on the award ceremony. In 1989 DJ Jazzy Jeff and the Fresh Prince (Will Smith) became the first Hip-Hop artists to win a Grammy for "Parents Just Don't Understand." On that same night, Kool Moe Dee became the first Hip- Hop artist to perform at the Grammy Awards. Young MC would be the first solo Hip-Hop artist to win an award in 1990. Queen Latifah and Salt-N-Pepa simultaneously became the first female artists to win a Grammy in 1995. Latifah won the best rap performance for a solo artist, and Salt-N-Pepa won the category for best group or duo. Naughty By Nature's *Poverty's Paradise* is the first Best Rap Album Grammy Award winner. Eminem's "Lose Yourself" was the first Best Rap Song Grammy in 2004. Lauryn Hill was the first rapper to win the Album of the Year Grammy in 1999. Outkast would become the first rap duo or group to win Album of the Year in 2004. In 1993, Arrested Development became the first rap artist to win the Best New Artist Grammy.

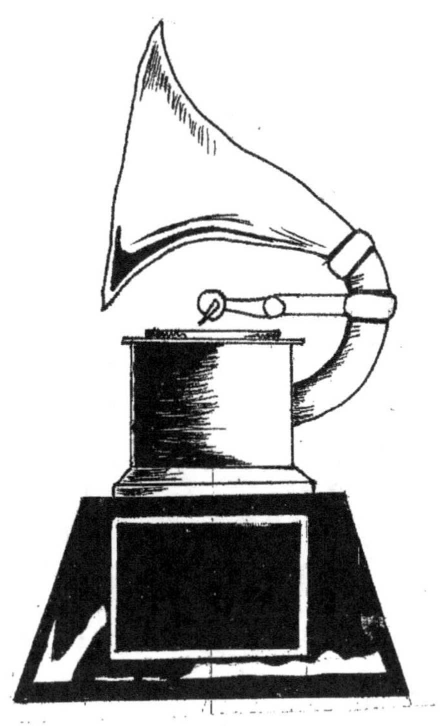

MC
HAMMER

Pp2
IS FOR PLEASE HAMMER DON'T HURT'EM

Please Hammer Don't Hurt 'Em is the first Hip-Hop album to be certified Diamond, which is 10 million units sold. Lauryn Hill's *Miseducation of Lauryn Hill* made her the first female rapper to be certified Diamond. Run DMC would be the first Hip- Hop act to be certified Gold and Platinum albums. Salt-N-Pepa are the first female Hip-Hop artists to be certified Platinum with their debut album *Hot, Cool & Vicious*. Da Brat is the first solo female Hip-Hop artist to go Platinum with her debut album *Funkdafied*. Kurtis Blow's "The Breaks" is the first Hip-Hop single to be certified Gold. Today, modern technology has impacted how music is purchased. Drake is the most streamed Hip-Hop artist with over 75 billion streams. Kanye West, Eminem, Juice WRLD, and XXXTentacion round up the top five most streamed Hip- Hop artists. Nicki Minaj is the most streamed female Hip-Hop artist.

Q1

IS FOR QUEEN LATIFAH

Queen Latifah is one of the most prolific and accomplished Hip-Hop artists to date. She is often referred to as the first lady of Hip-Hop. Queen Latifah is an activist, rapper, singer, actress, entrepreneur, and so much more. Latifah began her career as a rapper delivering Afrocentric consciousness. Queen Latifah became known for her lyrical content addressing sexism. Queen Latifah has an impressive resume as an actress in movies and television. Her acting career began to skyrocket after her role as Khadijah, a Hip-Hop entrepreneur, in the hit sitcom *Living Single*. Latifah also has credits as a producer and writer. She is the founder of Flavor Unit Entertainment and Management. Queen Latifah was the first female solo artist to win a Grammy award for "U.N.I.T.Y." in 1995. Latifah earned a Primetime Emmy award for her portrayal of Bessie Smith in 2015. Queen Latifah has also accumulated four BET Awards, four Image Awards, the Elle Women In Hollywood Icon Award, and an Essence Black Women in Hollywood Honoree. She received her star on the Hollywood Walk of Fame in 2006. In 2023 Queen Latifah became a Kennedy Center honoree. Queen Latifah supports Girl Up, GLAAD, Starlight Children's Foundation, and Dana-Farber Cancer Institute.

QUEEN
LATIFAH

Qq2

IS FOR LEE QUINONES

Lee Quinones (LEE) is a graffiti artist who has helped transition the street art form into popular culture circles. Quinones was born in Puerto Rico, but he was raised in the Lower East Side of New York. LEE would gain notoriety throughout New York for his works that covered entire subway cars. Around 1976 LEE began painting murals charged with political satire and fresh painting techniques. He would go on to star in the groundbreaking Hip-Hop film *Wild Style*. LEE has done several solo shows. His work has graced several international exhibits. His first exhibit was at Galleria Medusa in Rome, Italy. His work was featured in "Times Square Show" in 1980; "Graffiti Art Success for America at Fashion Moda" in 1980; and, in "Documenta #7" in Kassel, Germany in 1983. In recent years, LEE's work has been featured at the New Museum of Contemporary Art, The Museum of Modern Art, the Contemporary Art Center of Cincinnati, the Fun Gallery, and the Lisson Gallery to name a few. Lee Quinones lives and continues to work in Brooklyn, New York.

MC
SPRAY
CAN
DOPE

R1
IS FOR RAP MUSIC

On September 16, 1979, the entire world was introduced to Hip-Hop culture via rap music. "Rapper's Delight" was the first Hip-Hop single released by the Sugar Hill Gang. The Sugar Hill Gang consisted of Big Bank Hank, Wonder Mike, and Master Gee. Grand Master Caz was not credited for his writing contribution to Hank's rhymes. This single was a huge commercial success landing on Billboard's Top 40 chart. Today, "Rapper's Delight" is in the Library of Congress's National Recording Registry. Before the release of "Rapper's Delight", rap music was largely a local, underground passion. The release of "Rapper's Delight" was the catalyst for a cultural revolution. Hip-Hop culture would begin to spread like wildfire. The introduction of rap into the mainstream catapulted the MC into the forefront of the Hip-Hop movement. Jay-Z, Jermaine Dupri, Missy Elliott, and the Neptunes (Chad Hugo and Parrell Williams) have been inducted into the Song Writers Hall of Fame. Teddy Riley, who introduced the subgenre New Jack Swing, is also in the Song Writers Hall of Fame. Today, rap music is a global multibillion-dollar industry. Rap music is the most consumed genre of music in the United States. Rap music has penetrated every corner of the globe. The rap industry is extremely popular in the U.K., Canada, and Australia. The Netherlands, Korea, France, Russia, and Nigeria are just a few nations with their own variation of rap music. Rap music is so disproportionately more popular than the other elements of Hip-Hop that many mistakenly believe that rapping or emceeing is the only facet of Hip-Hop culture.

ROCK & ROLL
HALL OF FAME
ROCK AND ROLL
HALL OF FAME

Rr2
IS FOR ROCK &
ROLL HALL OF FAME

Rock and Roll music is significant to the American mainstream and global culture. By the 1950s, it dominated popular music. Rock and Roll embodies rebellion. It has proven to be inclusive to all ethnicities, races, creeds, classes, and spiritual backgrounds. Rock and Roll embodies many of the facets of Hip-Hop culture. It is without question that Rock and roll had an influence on the pioneers of Hip-Hop. After fifty years of existence, Hip-Hop artists are being recognized for their contributions to the Rock and Roll and popular music community. The following is a list of Hip-Hop artists inducted into the Rock and Roll Hall of Fame:

Grand Master Flash and the Furious Five	2007
Run-DMC	2009
The Beastie Boys	2012
Public Enemy	2013
N.W.A.	2016
2Pac	2017
The Notorious B.I.G.	2020
LL Cool J	2021
Jay-Z	2021
Eminem	2022
Missy Elliott	2023
DJ Kool Herc	2023

LONG LIVE ROCK

SOUL TRAIN

S1
IS FOR SOUL TRAIN

Soul Train played a role in spreading Hip-Hop culture throughout American popular culture. Soul Train was a dance television show created by the host Don Cornelius. It focused on the African-American viewing audience. The show received national syndication in 1971, featuring music and performances of the most popular R&B, soul, funk, and pop artists. By 1980 it would feature rap music as well. This was significant because Soul Train was already influencing Hip-Hop culture before Hip- Hop music became popular to the masses. Soul Train had a tremendous influence on street fashion and dance. As b-boying and b-girling were becoming popular in New York, a style of street dancing was developing by the Las Angeles street crews. Don Campbell and the Lockers introduced pop locking and other variations. Sam Solomon is credited for introducing the boogaloo style. Soul Train showcased these dance styles and played a role in enriching break dancing. Soul Train ran for 35 years. It played a huge part in showcasing Hip-Hop music, dance, and fashion for the vast majority of its air time.

Ss2
IS FOR SUGAR HILL RECORDS

Sugar Hill Records was the first rap music record label. It was established in 1979 by Sylvia Robinson. Robinson assembled Big Bank Hank, Wonder Mike, and Master Gee to create the rap group Sugar Hill Gang. Sugar Hill's release of "Rapper's Delight" had a profound impact on the spread of Hip-Hop culture. Primarily, the entire world was introduced to Hip-Hop music. Also, Robinson sparked the entrepreneurial machine that Hip-Hop culture would generate. As rap music became the voice of Hip-Hop, its practitioners became the face of Hip-Hop. The Hip-Hop elements of fashion and entrepreneurialism skyrocketed. Sugar Hill Records signed other acts such as Sequence, Grandmaster Flash and the Furious Five, and the Treacherous Three. Kurtis Blow would go on to be the first MC to sign with a major record label. MC Lyte was the first female MC to sign with a major record label.

TEMPLE OF
HIP-HOP
TEMPLE OF HIP HOP
VICTORY OVER THE STREETS
1996

T1
IS FOR TEMPLE OF HIP-HOP

The Temple of Hip-Hop is an international preservation society founded by Hip-Hop legend KRS-One. The Temple of Hip-Hop was founded in 1998. The Temple of Hip-Hop promotes the divinity of Hip-Hop culture. The Temple aims to continue to develop archives for the study of Hip Hop's history. The Temple aims to school and teach all interested in Hip Hop culture. The Temple of Hip-Hop aims to preserve Hip-Hop's original cause. The Temple of Hip-Hop played a vital role in the execution of the Hip-Hop Declaration of Peace, and the establishment of Hip-Hop Appreciation Week, which is celebrated the 3rd week of May. KRS-One is one of the most influential MCs whose content awakens political, social, spiritual, educational, and economic consciousness. He also spearheaded such projects as "Self-Destruction", in which the proceeds benefited the National Urban League. "Self Destruction" is a collaboration track with several of the finest Hip-Hop artists from the 1980s. KRS-One also organized Human Education Against Lies (HEAL) to bring consciousness to accurate and inclusive history.

T t2
IS FOR TOASTING

Toasting is a Jamaican style of deejaying that heavily influenced the development of Hip-Hop deejaying and emceeing. Rap standouts like Busta Rhymes, the late Heavy D, and the late Notorious B.I.G. are of Jamaican descent. Toasting gained momentum in the late 1960s and early 1970s. In Jamaica, travelling DJs with large speakers and elaborate sound systems were very popular. Toasting became a part of the musical entertainment. Toasting is a style of chanting. The Jamaican DJs engaged in chanting or talking over the music or drum beat. Toasting was usually done in a humdrum tone. Some toasting was improvised while others were scripted. Some toasts were comedic or boastful in nature. Others were storytelling put to rhymes. The travelling DJ would toast over the most popular hits and toast while selecting tracks. Toasting also influenced Dance hall artists such as Shabba Ranks, Shaggy, and Sean Paul.

U1
IS FOR UNIVERSAL HIP-HOP MUSEUM

The Universal Hip Hop Museum is located at 610 Exterior Street, Bronx, New York 10451. The museum is located in the birthplace of Hip-Hop culture. The mission of the Universal Hip-Hop Museum is to celebrate and preserve the history of local and global Hip-Hop music and culture to inspire, empower, and promote understanding. The museum was founded by Rocky Bucano with support from Hip- Hop icons Nas, LL Cool J, Ice T, and Kurtis Blow. The museum is set for 2024 opening.

LL COOL J

NEW YORK
BREAKDANCE

Uu2
IS FOR UNDISPUTED MASTERS

The Undisputed Masters is a global break dancing competition. It is a series of competitions that was established in 2014. The Undisputed Masters was established as a collaborative effort. Some of the world's most popular breaking events aligned judges and competitors to establish the Undisputed Masters. The Undisputed Masters has developed the judging system that will be used for the official scoring of the first Olympic breakdance competition in the Paris 2024 Olympic Games. The Undisputed Masters was established to connect the most popular competitions into a world series. Red Bull BC One, UK Championships, Battle of the Year, and R-16 Korea are the most popular international competitions. The most recent Masters events took place in London, Amsterdam, Los Angeles, and Tokyo. Some of the world's best b-boys and b-girls competing in international competitions are Wizard (CAN), Victor (USA), Menno (HOL), Jilou (Ger), and Nicka (LIT).

VIDEO
MUSIC BOX

V1
IS FOR VIDEO MUSIC BOX

*V*ideo *Music Box* helped popularize Hip-Hop music and culture throughout New York, and it set the blueprint to further propel Hip-Hop to the American mainstream. *Video Music Box* was established by Ralph McDaniels, a communications major from Queens, New York. He is affectionately known as Uncle Ralph. Through the platform of his show, he was able to help launch the careers of rappers and Hip-Hop fashion entrepreneurs. *Video Music Box is* often aired from local clubs and other community locations. This contributed to McDaniels' authenticity. McDaniels also used his platform to address community and social issues that impacted the Hip-Hop community. *Video Music Box* popularized the "shoutout" and Hip-Hop vernacular. Ralph McDaniels and his co-host Vid Kid (Lionel Martin) paved the way for such shows as *Yo MTV Raps* and *Rap City. You're Watching Video Music Box* is a documentary directed by legendary Hip- Hop MC, Nas, which tells the story of the impact of Ralph McDaniel and his groundbreaking show. Uncle Ralph continues to advocate for Hip-Hop culture.

Vv2
IS FOR THE VILLAGE VOICE

The Village Voice played a role in establishing Hip-Hop as one of the most popular cultures in the United States. The Village Voice is a periodical founded in 1955. The Village Voice is known for its coverage of the culture, politics, and street life of New York City. It was founded by Dan Wolf, John Wilcock, and Norman Mailer. The Village Voice is known for its coverage of New York's vast cultural diversity. On September 21, 1982, Steven Hager published an article titled " Afrika Bambaataa's Hip Hop." This was the first publication of the term "Hip Hop."

WILD STYLE

W1
IS FOR WILD STYLE

Wild *Style* helped introduce the Hip-Hop way of life throughout the United States and around the globe. *Wild Style* is regarded as the first Hip-Hop movie, showcasing the connection of the elements of Hip-Hop. Many of the early practitioners of Hip-Hop culture were featured in the film such as Grandmaster Flash, Grand Wizard Theodore, Rock Steady Crew, the Cold Crush Brothers, Fab 5 Freddy, DONDI, and ZEPHYR. This film ushered in opportunities for Hip-Hop artists in Hollywood. Hip-Hop artists would begin to land roles in movies and television shows. Today, Hip-Hop artists have ascended to become box office blockbusters. Many have become writers, producers, and directors. Hip-Hop culture is featured in movies, sitcoms, prime-time dramas, and reality TV.

Ww2
IS FOR WILL SMITH

Will Smith may be the most accomplished Hip-Hop entertainer in America and throughout the entire world. Will Smith is a rapper, actor, author, humanitarian, and entrepreneur. Will Smith began his career as an MC. DJ Jazzy Jeff and the Fresh Prince (Will Smith) wasted no time climbing the rap charts and accumulating countless accolades. Smith's charisma and positive image made his transition into television and movies very smooth. He became an American household name in the lead role of the television show *The Fresh Prince of Bel-Air*. He has sold over 12 million albums worldwide. As a leading actor, Will Smith's movies have generated over $6 billion worldwide making him a box office smash. His music career has earned him five American Music Awards, four Grammy Awards, and five VMAs. As an actor, Will Smith won the Oscar for Best Performance by an Actor in a Leading Role in the film *King Richard*. Smith has also racked up four BET awards, one Golden Globe, and five NAACP Image Awards. Will Smith is an author of three books, of which one is a children's book. Will Smith is known for supporting charities such as the Will and Jada Smith Family Foundation, Dream Foundation, and Living Classrooms Foundation.

WILL SMITH

HIP·HOP ON A HIGHER LEVEL
FEBRUARY 2000
XXL
DMX
DEAD MAN WALKING
MASTER P
Mo' Money, Mo' Haters
RAEKWON'S
Secret Recipe
Goodie Mob
New World Pop-A-Ganda
THE LOX
Life After Puff
KORUPT
BARKS BACK
DR. DRE'S
COMEBACK
ALBUM
GRANDMASTER
FLASH
MYSTIKAL
M.O.P.
PHAROAHE
MONCH
$MOSDEF
TWO TIMES DOPE
SHUT 'EM DOWN
AMERICA'S WAR ON PROJECTS
XXL #15
11-30-30 OUR PRICE $3.77
195368-6

X1
IS FOR XXL MAGAZINE

XXL magazine and the Source magazine are two of the most popular magazines providing news, photos, interviews, and critiques of the most current Hip-Hop music and its artists. Both magazines are based out of New York. XXL was founded in 1997 by Aiden James, Michael Luna, O'Neal Anthony Josiah, and Xzander B. XXL currently publishes monthly and has a website. The magazine became extremely popular for its freshman class covers where the magazine spotlights ten up-and-coming Hip-Hop artists. The Source is the oldest Hip-Hop periodical and started as a newsletter back in 1988. The Source was founded by Dave Mays. The Source currently publishes annually and has a website. The magazine was notorious for its five-microphone rating scale for Hip-Hop albums. At its peak, The Source also hosted a highly anticipated awards show for Hip-Hop music.

THE SOURCE

XXXTENTACION

Xx2
IS FOR XXXTENTACION

The late XXXTentacion was a rapper who made an impact on the American mainstream, and his legacy continues to grow five years after his death. As a musician, he pushed the boundaries of traditional Hip-Hop music. His music carved out its own space openly addressing depression and suicidal thoughts. XXXTentacion embraced distortion in his production, and his music gained even more popularity in the wake of his death. XXXTentacion is praised for his musical influence by Kendrick Lamar, Ye, and the late Juice WRLD. He is credited with over 45 million units sold worldwide. XXXTentacion has won one American Music Award and one BET Hip-Hop Award. His critics condemn him due to acts of violence in his personal life. However, XXXTentacion's supporters praise him for his openness in his personal fight against mental illness. Many of his fans claim that he has helped them in their struggle against mental illness through his music and availability via social media. XXX is extremely popular among Generation Y (Millennials) and Generation Z. In his short 20 years on earth, XXXTentacion made a profound impact on mental health awareness.

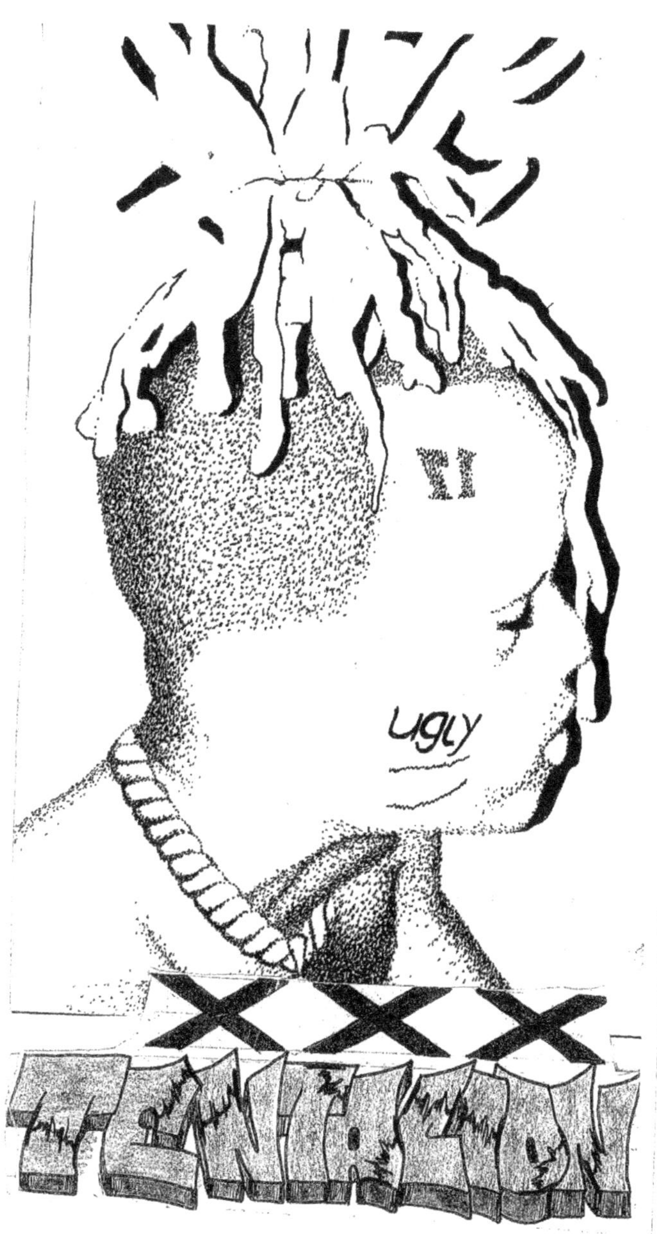

HI
UGLY

Y1
IS FOR GENERATION Y (MILLENNIALS)

The Millennials are currently the most influential age group in the current Hip-Hop scene. Many of the pioneers of Hip-Hop culture fall in the baby boomer and Generation X category. The baby boomers and Gen X are transitioning to late and middle adulthood. The largest consumers of Hip-Hop music fall in the age range of 16-24 years of age. Millennials and Generation Z fall into this stage of young adulthood and adolescence.

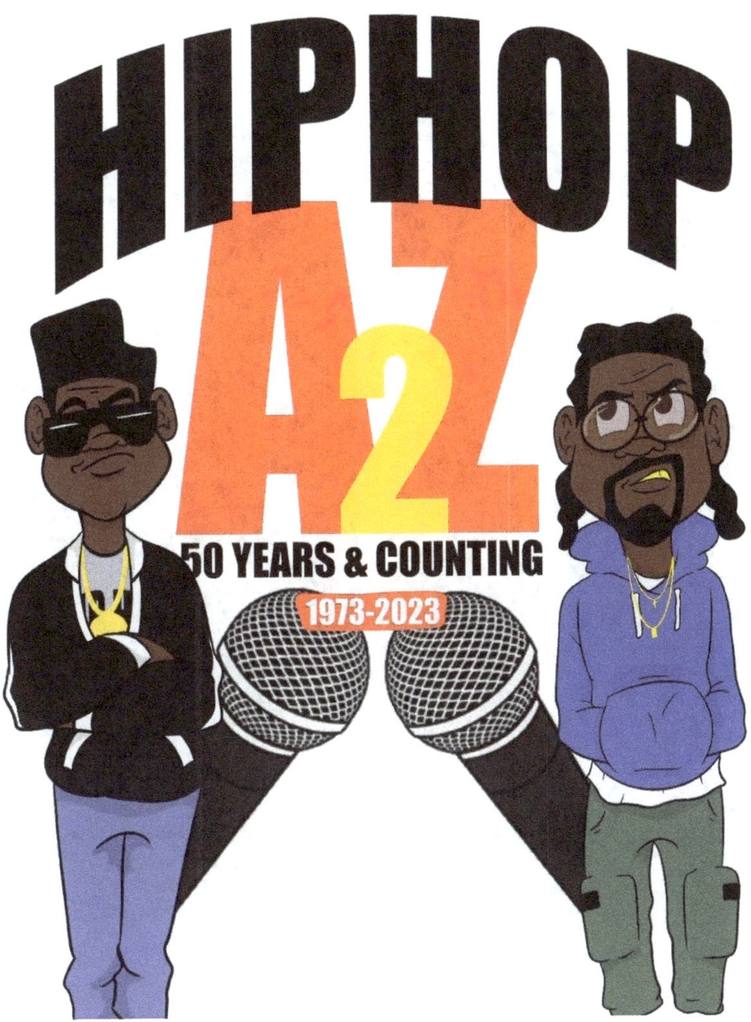
HIPHOP
A2Z
50 YEARS & COUNTING
1973-2023

YO

Yy2
IS FOR YO

Yo is a word commonly used in the Hip-Hop community. It was frequently used by MCs to gain the attention of the party crowd or listeners. In conversation, it can be used as an expression of excitement or as a greeting. MTV further popularized the term by using it in the title of *Yo! MTV Raps.* This is an example of street language. Street language is an element of Hip-Hop culture. Hip-Hop culture continuously creates the slang and jargon that influences mainstream society. MTV's incorporation of the word "yo" is just one example.

YO!
MAD SKILLS
DOWN
MY BAD
SLAMMIN'
WORD
DUDE!
SWEET
FRESH
DOPE!
WACK
TIGHT
COOL
WHATCHA!
CLUTCH
BLING
SKILL!
STREET
LANGUAGE
HOT
PLACE
BUGGIN
DUH!
FLY
AIIIGHT! WHAT UP DOH!?
DHAT

Z1

IS FOR ZULU BEATS

Zulu Beat was one of the earliest pure Hip-Hop shows on commercial radio. The show was launched on the New York radio station WHBI. The show was hosted by DJ Afrika Islam and Donald D. DJ Red Alert would eventually host also. *Zulu Beat* was preceded by John "Mr. Magic" Rivas' *Rap Attack*. It aired on WBLS in May of 1982. Marley Marl was Mr. Magic's co-host. In 1983 Los Angeles radio station KDAY 1580-AM became the first Hip-Hop radio station courtesy of music director Greg Mack. Today, Sirius XM has several stations dedicated to Hip-Hop music. Rock the Bells Radio, Hip-Hop Nation, and Shade 45 are a few. Roxanne Shante, Sha Rock, Bun B, DJ Whoo Kid, DJ Drama, Sway, and Nina 9 are some of the hosts and DJs that deliver Hip-Hop programming.

A
RAP ATTACK
A
Zulu Beats

zephyr

Zz2
IS FOR ZEPHYR

Zephyr is one of the most popular graffiti artists in America and beyond. He grew up in Manhattan. He was attracted to street art at a very early age. Zephyr began to hang out with a street art crew by the name of the Rolling Thunder Writers. He gained popularity by tagging his street art name, Zephyr, on subway trains. Zephyr borrowed his name from a popular surfboard brand. He was featured in the movie *Wild Style* and the documentary *Style Wars*. His work has been featured at 17 Frost Gallery, the Museum of Graffiti (Miami), and the Museum of Street Art in New York.

ABOUT THE AUTHOR

Robert Waugh is an intervention specialist and advocate for special education. He was born in Cleveland, Ohio. Mr. Waugh obtained his Bachelor's and Master's degree from Cleveland State University where he majored in history and special education respectively. Mr. Waugh has twenty-four years of teaching experience. He has taught in Cleveland and Warrensville Heights. Mr. Waugh has many years of experience as a coach of football, basketball, wrestling, and track & field. Robert Waugh is a proud member of the Omega Psi Phi Fraternity Inc. and a Prince Hall Mason. Mr. Waugh is a Hip Hop enthusiast and fan.

SHOUTOUTS

Donya L. Waugh Robert "Suave" Waugh II "Ill Dyl" Dylon L. Waugh Davenport Waugh Norma Waugh Herbie Waughbanger Herbie Herb Lori Waugh Brevin Waugh Brandon Waugh Sean Waugh Wicked Life Stephanie Waugh Fatback Band Scarface Willie D Bushwick Bill Devin the Dude J Prince Scott La Rock Rick Rubin Rakim Talib Kweli Mos Def Redman Method Man Wu-Tang EPMD Big Daddy Kane Dolemite Guru DJ Premier Jam Master J Pete Rock DJ Khaled Kid Capri Spinderella Diamond Cuts Big Pun Fat Joe Kool G Rap TI Tribe Called Quest Dungeon Family UTFO Whodini EPMD 8Ball & MJG UGK Native Tongue The Roots X-Clan Dead Prez Lupe Fiasco Jadakiss E 40 Big Lil Wayne Gucci Mane Young Jeezy Rick Ross Future Wale Big Sean Killer Mike Lil Kim YoYo Foxy Brown Trina Megan Thee Stallion Eve Cardi B Rapsody Lady of Rage Sister Souljah Latto Cochise Johnny O Casper C MC Chill Lord Jazz Bone Thugs N Harmony MC Brains Kid Cudi Machine Gun Kelly Ray Cash Bankie Travolta Al Fatz Chip Tha Ripper EC Marv Big Topic Foreign Jay Baebae Savo Ripp Flamez Brothers 4 the Struggle Nerve DJs Lady Skills Joe X DJ Ellery Smooth MC Serge Shock Kid Pierre DJ Supreme P.I.M.P. Lon T Cock Diesel Jay Kool Doc B & Mic D Doc Scout Derrie Doc Roel Bango the B-Boy Outlaw III Style Rockers Mister Soul Ranger Sano Poke Suave Goddi Dre Live Ski Forrest Getum Gump Mix Master Fresh Lyricist JD Cleveland Assasin Rev Bandit Versatile Mother Rapper Poet Darryl Adams Paul Broxton Swipe R Gates Sammy D Steve Hendrix Doc Rock Grand

Master Smooth Nic Rebel John J DJ Chill DJ DNyce Wicked
Picket Shawn Twaun Lashawn Moore Skills Lo Key Blend T
Bone Steady Pace Indica Spitts Tripple Threat Tri-X Praise
Money 6 Pack Spoony T Top Cat Prime K Wall Keith Success
Shawn Smith Nate the Great Lay Low D Law Joe Simpty
Shawn C Kevvy Kev Rell E Rell DJ Scratch Master Lo Lo
Corey Jones Walter Filmore Darian Savage